ANiMAL TAiLS

Ray James

Rourke
Publishing LLC
Vero Beach, Florida 32964

www.rourkepublishing.com

PHOTO CREDITS: All photos © Lynn M. Stone.

Title page: The snow leopard has a long, furry tail.

Editor: Robert Stengard-Olliges

Cover design by Nicola Stratford.

Library of Congress Cataloging-in-Publication Data

James, Ray
  Animal tails / Ray James.
     p. cm. -- (Let's look at animals)
  Includes index.
  ISBN 1-60044-167-X (Hardcover)
  ISBN 1-59515-528-7 (Softcover)
  1. Tails--Juvenile literature. I. Title. II. Series: James, Ray. Let's
look at animals.
  QL950.6.S76 2007
  591.4--dc22
                            2006013009

Printed in the USA

CG/CG

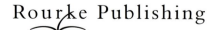

Rourke Publishing

www.rourkepublishing.com – sales@rourkepublishing.com
Post Office Box 3328, Vero Beach, FL 32964

Table of Contents

Many Different Tails 4

Useful Tails 10

Tails Can Talk 14

Tails on the Move 18

Glossary 23

Index 24

Many Different Tails

Many kinds of animals have tails. Tails may be short or long. Tails come in many sizes and shapes.

The ring-tailed **lemur's** tail is longer than its body.

4

A tail may be long and round, like an otter's tail. It may be wide and flat, like a beaver's tail. The tail supports the beaver while it works.

A tail may be covered with fur, like a dog's. A fish tail is covered with scales. A wolf's tail is fluffy.

A tail may have long feathers, like a peacock's tail. A tail may have long, sharp **quills**, like a porcupine's tail.

Useful Tails

Animals use their tails in many ways. A woodpecker's tail is stiff. It is good support when the bird hammers a tree.

Whales swim with their tails. Their wide tails also help them dive deep into the ocean. Whale tails are called **flukes**.

Monkeys and lemurs have long tails. Their tails work almost like long fingers! They can curl their tails around branches. Some monkeys can even hang by their tails!

12

Tree squirrels are climbers, too. Squirrels and many other animals use their tails for balance.

Tails Can Talk

Cats and dogs move their tails to help show how they feel. A happy dog may wag its tail.

Many male birds use their tail feathers to show off for females. Tom turkeys show off for hen turkeys.

Even snakes have tails. The tip of a rattlesnake tail is very unusual. It can make a buzzing sound. The buzz warns of danger.

Tails on the Move

Birds' tails help them fly well. A bird uses tail feathers to help change direction or speed. The eagle's long tail feathers help it turn during flight.

Alligators and crocodiles have long, powerful tails. They move their tails to swim. An alligator can whip its tail quickly.

Fish also use their tails to swim. Female **salmon** even use their tails to dig out little nests in stream bottoms. The mother salmon lays her eggs in the nest.

Glossary

fluke (FLOOK) – the tail of a whale

lemur (LEE mur) – any one of several furry, tree-climbing animals that are cousins of monkeys

quill (KWIL) – the long, stiff, and sharp hairs of a porcupine

salmon (SAM uhn) – a kind of fish born in fresh water but that grows up in the ocean

Index

lemur   4, 12
long   4, 6, 8
swim   11, 20, 22
tree   12, 13
wag   14

FURTHER READING

Hall, Peg. *Whose Tail Is This?*. Picture Window Books, 2003.

Jenkins, Steve. *What Do You Do With A Tail Like This?*. Houghton Mifflin, 2003.

WEBSITES TO VISIT

http://www.newton.dep.ani.gov/askasci/zoo00/zoo00557.htm

ABOUT THE AUTHOR

Ray James writes children's fiction and nonfiction. A former teacher, Ray understands what kids like to read. Ray lives in Gary, Indiana with his wife and three cats.